Releasing Birds

Poems by
Lisa Spears

FREE VERSE PRESS

A FREE VERSE, LLC EXPERIENCE

The author is available for performances. If interested, please email **follypoet63@gmail.com.**

ISBN: 979-8-9871632-8-3

Library of Congress Control Number: 2023947880

Design by Marcus Amaker
Artwork by Boston Public Library / Unsplash
Author photo by Jason Layne

Printed in the United States of America.
First printing edition 2023.

Published by Free Verse Press
Free Verse, LLC
North Charleston, South Carolina
freeversepress.com

Artwork by Elyahna Miller

This book was written in honor of my mother and my dream of long ago.
It is dedicated with love and joy to my daughters and granddaughters...
Angel and Hope
Elyahna, Melody, and Sunny

Thanks be to God.

Acknowledgements

This book has evolved from my essay "The Cross at Yellow Brick Road." In that work, I put on my Mother's shoes and traveled her 'yellow brick road' shortly after her passing (1999).

The whole world shifted for me, "...I saw it black and white before...death can breathe." I went after everything...in color~ for both of us.

Along my road, I had my own scarecrows, tin men, and lions to help guide and inspire me.

I want to thank Prof. Judy Straffin from Rock Valley College who saw that essay to the finish. She called me a "writer" and encouraged me to apply to a university. I found my place in academia at Western Illinois University and met Prof. David Stevenson while working on my Master's of English. He is a great writer of fiction, was supportive of my work, guided me through my master's thesis, and would later write my recommendations for an MFA program. I also want to thank Prof. Marjorie Allison. I took every class she taught in literature and felt the shape of words in a multicultural context. I was conversing with the world and never wanted to leave school.

I have to create a separate space of thanks for my poetry professors at Eastern Washington University. Through the guidance of Prof. Jonathan Johnson and Prof. Christopher Howell, I found a window to my soul's calling and a way to answer it. I could listen to the birds and let them go. Prof. Johnson has remained an inspiring mentor and friend. His influence is immeasurable, and words cannot convey how often I recalled his encouragement in quiet hours of writing.

I want to thank all of my people on Folly Beach and my first open mics—from the audience who listened, to an array of artists/musicians that welcomed me and heard this book in sections to the completion of a dream. To the sea of Folly that brings me back to myself when I lose my way; you are the compass of God's infinity.

To my publisher (Free Verse Press) and friend, Marcus Amaker, I was drawn to his work before our first meeting and taught his poetry to my students. Now, through his support, this book has brought me to 'somewhere over the rainbow.' I am beyond grateful to him and look forward to the road ahead of our connection and collaboration as poets.

To my family~ you will always be my house and 'there is no place like home.'

"The sky is everywhere,
it begins at our feet."~Jandy Nelson

Table of Contents

My Mother Making an Entrance

Standing at the prison gate
I thought her the most beautiful.
Beyond my seven years
I knew it was so.

Like Marilyn Monroe or Elizabeth Taylor
running late to that cocktail party at
a quarter past three,

Her headscarf in a loose knot
of light sheer pink
rustles in the wind.

She is a tall 5'2
and gently brushes back
the unruly strand
that wraps around her finger.

I know when she reached heaven's gate
the angels cleaned the spatters
of my father's sins
from her light blue dress.

The Dove has brought her tears
to me in a bottle.

I call them words.

Frames

In all of our travels
we lost our childhood photos.

Some were on the trail
of cars repossessed,
others locked in evictions.

There is one.

I am a baby
Dad is holding me.

Mom is touching
the hem of my dress,

As if we are still
connected,

Sustaining each other
for a life we couldn't
picture.

The Labor in Delivery

In New Orleans my sister was born.
In pains my Mother circles the Mardi Gras.
In the taxi the meter is ticking.
In the window all the people are dancing.

In the hospital my Mother who is Judy is Mrs. Billie Jean.
In the room she cries for my Grandma Eileen.
In the stirrups she is still on the run.
In the hall is my Father with a fake beard and glasses.
In his pocket a loaded gun.

In Kentucky he shot a cop dead.
In the U.S. he is the Top Ten Most Wanted.
In February it is the twentieth.
In the hotel I am five years old waiting.

Out comes a baby.
I love my sister so.

Sketch

First, Mom drew the outline,
and it was a perfect likeness
of suburban life in the seventies.

A small house, a
cloudless sky, a
weeping willow, a
car in the drive,

A few kids, a
white picket fence, a
porch framed with morning glory flowers.

She must have drawn
that picture for hours.

Everything was standing in the distance.

The Code

I spent a lot of time at Kent State.
That's the pen and not the school.

It was there I learned the lingo.
Where rat, pig, snitch,
and in the hole
began to take form.

I was the daughter of #K07594, and
I took that responsibility seriously.

Visiting was a duty,
often times a present
for Christmas or my birthday.

On a road of uncertainty,
this trip had certain formalities
The givens, what I did know,
what could be counted on.

First, the drive was long.
Five hundred and three miles
is quite a stretch, so
Dad did time,
I did distance.

That big house sure looked majestic,
all sparkly in nature by a shimmering lake.
It almost tricked me
everytime we rounded the curve..

A closer inspection revealed
it's true character.

Stone faced guards
with jingling keys,
to frisk my Mother,
and sometimes me.

Drafty hallways
encased in concrete,
forever sunless,

With the resounding echo of
open, shut, bang,
open, shut, bang.

Then, there he stood
in tan uniform, and
we dressed like Sunday
no matter the day of the week.

And, I would listen to
the huddled conversations
between my parents when they thought
I wasn't listening.

They thought I was wiping slobber
off of my baby brother, or
nursing my wounded knee.

That's how I knew
that Panky never ratted,
that they never found the gun,

That a pretty boy was shanked
for putting the finger on so and so,
that a hole wasn't in the ground.

It was my way of being
on the inside
when most of life was on the out.

I answered questions like expected,
life was fine, and
school was good.

I had to protect my father
from the harsh realities
of the outside world.

It was a job
I had assigned myself early on.

I gave it all up
when he came home.

For awhile, after his release
life seemed normal.

He took me skating,
told me to turn my music down,
went to parent's night at school.

Until the whispers started.
Some things are set in stone.

It threw me a little off balance
to learn that strangers
never crossed him, or

He'd burn the house down,
throw them in the river,
or poison the dog.

I shook things off,
didn't listen,
cause I knew the code.

Life is fine, and
school is good.

To even things out
I smoked a few joints
took a pill… or two.

It wasn't enough,
I needed to prove myself,
Once, and for all.

So, I picked a fight with a girl
who bullied me at school.

Held a garden spade
above her,
felt the coolness
in my hand,

Then, I let it fall
to the left of me,

On the green, green ground.

I cried, and
crawled out of the hole.

I went to visit him in prison
the year I turned thirty-five.

Nothing looked familiar.
None of the old rules applied.

He was an old man
needing forgiveness
before he died.

It was the right thing to do.

The Teeing Ground

The brick house on the corner of Route 29 stood vacant.
The yard was impeccably neat, and
seemed to weed and mow itself.

It's only flaw was a silvery propane gas tank
centered near perfect in the backyard.
An occasional daisy grew up the side,
never enough to decorate it.

That corner became our rest stop
on long walks to the golf course.
No, we were not avid golfers,
only four children of a single mother.

Summer was the best season
so, we would offer our help,
wading to the knee in makeshift ponds
looking for golf balls.

We would fill the bucket to the brim,
then, Mom would place it in the stroller basket
with baby Sis for the long walk home.

One approaching spring,
a mother bird took up residence
at the top of that silvery tank.

Remnants of that nest
spilled from the top
like a makeshift hat.

We would race to that corner backyard
through the byway reeds and

raise the silver top.

Mom's admonishment to never
touch an egg or a feather
stayed fresh in my mind,

Like the blue of her eyes
when they flew away.

Prayer Practice

Our Father, my Mother said was how you begin to pray, and she gave me the shape of the world in my outstretched hands.

She said President Kennedy was shot like the Lennon John, and, then another man named King and streets were flooded with so many tears of all the people, and when I was born I only weighed two lbs. and my Grandma caught a bus every day to light a candle and make me a miracle.

She said that the POWs in Vietnam were scared and alone, and they were somebody's brother, father, or son, and that we had plenty to be together and have pancakes for supper, and someday we might have a color T.V. to watch "The Wizard of Oz."

She said my dad had done something wrong, and that's why he was in prison, and it was okay to still love and try to forgive him, and that I should try not to complain on our walk to the pond because we were all girls and my brother didn't have a man to take him fishing.

She said it was getting late, and I looked past the ceiling to what would be the stars to finish praying, and I knew there were angels watching her watch me, and Thine Was The Glory.

The Pack

Although there must have been color,
I only remember white that winter.
It was almost as if
we didn't exist at all
if not for the stray dogs.

They saw three kids, a woman, and a wagon,
saw our silhouettes in the snow,
and began to follow us,

Then, to take the lead
through drifts and ditches
past McClelland farm,
up and over
the cemetery hill,

Until, we could feel
the glistening,
until we could see
the light
of the corner IGA.

Casting Hearts and Stones

"Flat rocks are best" I told the boy
who saw me playing alone
kid lost in the crowd of the concrete
schoolyard blues to be the new girl
again in scuffed up shoes head down
hopping the scotch of squares in
Irving town the name of my third
fourth grade school.

I was like Saul on the road
to Demascus changing my mind
about boys because Paul smiled down
asking "Is this rock right?"

In that bright light I skippity-soared
across the calendar week above
the sneers and the jeers felt
cursive in the L of my name.

At the Woolworth's five and dime I struck
out to find him the goldest
fish for his bowl and parting
the sea of shyness stood

At his front door with fins
in a plastic bag of water when
he said they were moving handing
me the stone of sweetest sorrow.

Releasing Birds

Lately, I've been counting birds.
A Rosella, Robin, and Red-Wing a many.
The Sapphire, Sparrow, Snowfinch, and Swallow
to name a few.
I can see their indelible patterns, shapes in the vast sky.
Look! They hover just above the rim
of my childhood.
The house is small and gray-shingled,
blustery,
like it could be rain.

I am there
at nine years old
the little keeper
of so many siblings.

They have found a baby bird
taking shallow breaths,
with a tiny, yellow beak,
open-mouthed,
no sound.
They put it in a box.
When they are all nested,
the house is fast asleep,
I am haunted
by their catch, and
devise its release.
The moon hangs low,
I run along a silver path
to a tree with open limbs
then, I place the little bird
onto the long, soft grass.

I will return
my mind there
a thousand times ten

I am only eighteen
Mom has bipolar; and
she is sick again.

The state has come
to take my siblings, and
the sky is falling.

Sister circling memories
baby birds in my chest,
Run to me
brown eyed brother
see me walking after school.
Here, middle sis
let me lace those shoes.
Baby Sue can't find my hair
to twist with little fingers,

She's afraid of the dark
open mouth,
no sound.

Circling,
The state has taken
little hands to keep warm
in my pockets.
Falling,
hopscotch with
squiggly lines, balls
and jacks and
wagon rides.

Flailing,
Up doorsteps and byways and low ways and sideways
the state took
everything,
every morning.
For over a decade
in offices, wrong houses,
on the phone
I wait.
It's my brother, dear brother
he plays football
for Kansas state.

A little bird flew
from my chest
as I held his grown face.
I didn't stop
until I set every bird free.

Baby Sue
was last
how she'd waited for me.
Twelve fosters and a worn teddy bear,
Circling, circling, circling
we were finally all there.

Now, there is Sarha, Steven, Fayth, Nevaeh,
Nicholas and Syairi.
David, Mary Bernadette, Philomena, Teresa, and
Joseph. Then, comes Marie and Paige, followed
by Susan (also known as Elcee) Kenny, Zyonna
and Beth. There's Angel, Elyahna, Hope, Melody,
and the baby, Sunny.

Me, I lead from behind
our silhouette in the sky.
Look, there's a tree with arms open wide.

Ode to Eternity

The dress was the lightest of tans
with a touch of spring flowers.

I waited on the knell of the hour
for help from my sisters to
dress my dead Mother.

Not one for detail, yet
I have turned a funeral home
into a beauty parlor.

It took the three of us
to drape the dress
over her head and
pull her arms through the sleeves.

Her brows had to be arched…just so,
a dab of blush for the cheeks,
and a faint lip color.

I held her head
so they could clasp
the tiny cross necklace.

We shared a bit of gossip
and laughed at having
almost forgotten her undergarments.

I waved my sisters on to handle
the other tasks at home.

Outside, the birds sang
the setting sun kept time to
our last afternoon.

Then, I folded my Mother's hands.

I had done for her
what she had done for me
a thousand times.

Now, I see her face
when I get ready.

For Mike Kaufman
In Honor of~7/14/21
before & after

Perpetuity

Such is the beauty
in life,
just when we think
we can't hold
anymore,

Our arms open again
like perennials.

Give me the annual
frosts,
the seasonal
rains,

Lest, I forget the
warmth
In the east rising
suns, and

When it is dark
my friend,

I will

Hold
onto the stars
of love's full
bloom.

For Mike Martin & Mason

Listen to the Boy

In twilight fold
between bended day and night
I rise in restlessness, and
the silence of the world
it answers me.

Beyond obscurity,
there at the window sill,
I have a vision
of an Indiana town.

There is a boy there
who speaks without words
who shall lead them.

The soul stirs long before
a finger grazes the string
of a holy instrument.

He is there
on a back country road
riding a three wheeled bike
all cares abandoned.

An uncle's loving charge,
a boy with the world in his eye,
and the wind in his hair,
he listens,

To the seed
in barren field,
the circular moon
of a sparrow's nest,

To the mighty oak
her arms uplifted,
awaiting those wings of return.

Listen!
To the green, green grass
and the wild yellow flowers,
and the pure reflection of
clouds on water.

Span a life,
span an hour, and
the boy will go the distance,

And, the uncle will follow
as he tells him of
a better way home.

For: Dan Clamp
With Abiding Prayer
For Him and His Mother, Pat
1/15/2023

Where Dandelions Bloom

186,000 miles is the speed of light
and just to the other side
a timeless realm.
The place where our days
are not numbered.

"As it was in the beginning,
Is now, and
ever shall be."

I wish we could ride
a bend of light
on a morning sun.

I would grab your hand,
and we would visit
that crystal river.

Maybe then, your fears
would not feel
as certain.

Yet, we are bound to earth,
and God in His glory
gives us glimpses
beyond heaven's gate.

Like the first time
you kissed my cheek, or
when I saw your soul
there on a Sunday's
third row of a church pew.

Rest assured that by
His hand your Mother
has them, too.

Your first cry
rings out every mid-
September, and a fistfull of
dandelions still bloom.

The tunes from your first guitar
even now they carry
from the front porch
to the heart's living room.

She will ever be
the frame of life's doorway
calling you home, and

The first and the last note
of your songs to the Lord
from a church organ.

186,000 miles per second
is the speed of light.

Surely, I have known you
in God's time,
on His earth,
through this dark night.

My prayers for you
unfurled
among the stars.

Among the lines
I wish you might feel
my hope
in heaven's
boundless
reflection.

At 3:16 a.m.

… It's not quite yesterday and not yet today…

and I think it is a good place to be and I want to
make the most of it and my children and their
children are good and if you pulled up a chair
you might notice that there are books I've read
long ago strewn about because the best lines
remind me that I am a woman in the making and
there will always be a remainder to carry over to
the next afternoon and you might find me there
sad and joyful and sane and crazy and perhaps
it's all beautiful to know me and not know me
and I might kiss a stranger or not just to surprise
myself and across the way while you are sleeping
I think of you and how you multiplied the sun and
the moon and brought me closer to myself beyond
all distances and when I write my name in the sand I
understand and I will walk barefoot into everything
and I believe that is the best solution and I vow to
only laugh more and cry more and hug the sky
more and pray that I make it count more and the
more I love I love.

All the King's Horses
(and)
What Can't Be Put Back Together Again

The mind is a fragile thing
I bore witness
with six year old eyes
to its greatness, and
its demise.

My Mother's innocence was
not of this world, and
my father's greatest crime
was bringing her down to earth

With heavy fists and
loaded guns, and her
own street corner,
the price of an open mouth.

After his arrest, she
resurrected rainbows, roses, and
a red breasted robin.
She taught me to walk in the garden.

Soon, she began that ascent
to the stars, conversing
with holy angels in gibberish
unclothed, hands lifted.

She left on a stretcher like a
strapped rubber doll to
the state asylum gallows.

In time, she would return
to gather her children
under her wing,
happy tears and fly away home.

Our three heads lay on
her chest, her heart,
her house breathing.

I, as the oldest child
devised a plan
to build a fortress,
hold all invaders at bay.

Once the walls of silence were secure,
I put on my armor and doubled
playing hopscotch and sentry guard.

Careful, Mom is there weeping
She's reaching for the stars
in our enchanted garden.

The saints are marching in
again,
her mind floats
somewhere far above.

She will beat the devil
black and blue
out of me,
"He must go out of you!"

Be strong, be brave, be true

I will help gather our provisions,
pack up the car
toys, dog, and children.

We moved over thirty times in nine years.
We just kept running
from voices or watered down
versions of my Father.

By the time I was eighteen,
she had lost my siblings, and
homelessly wandered the streets.

After she died, I learned
a Mother's love far outweighs
an imbalance of the mind.

I threw down my armor, and
gathered her voice like a ribbon
to wrap around me.

It tells me that I am all things good.

The Champions

That fall we were in training,
there on the 3rd floor
of the corner building
at the crossroad
between 6th and East State.

It was life on life's terms,
a 30 day obstacle course
without the score of booze, a line, or a fix.

As starters, we were pale, tired, sickly.
Some had shakes, sores, or tracks.

Most of us had the clothes on our backs,
and more baggage than we could carry.

We wore fronts in layers to disguise depths of despair.
These facades were interchangeable,
but we all had a main cover.

Tracy might punch your face if you looked twice,
Russ was the peacemaker,
Betty told blackout stories that could keep us in stitches,
and me, you know, I kept my eyes on the floor.

You, Phil Avigliano, you hid behind that Italian debonair.
You could make a Pall Mall look good,
hands dancing like a maestro—
guiding words through the air.

It must have been around the 5th day,
I was lost in my mind and tripped into you.

"Yo, Adrian," you said with a smile.

I thought you were being an ass because I had way more
spunk than Talia Shire in that movie,

for one–for two… then,
you grabbed my hand,
and it took.

It took me to the other side of endless routines
up at 6:00, lines for B12 and tests for Hep B, meetings and
counseling, busting ghosts from the past, and we kissed in
the stairwell and swore that off because we wouldn't mess
each other up and

Week 3 and the park and the color of leaves,
a chill in the breeze, and
"Yo, you can hit the ball,"
you are cheering,
and the sun on our face and we're laughing,

"Look, Phil,...We are living!"

The last week is the hardest of an uphill climb,
time to tell my story,
in a few days say goodbye.

Our group is in a circle and I am turning pages,
reading the shape of twenty-four years hell bent on hiding,
and then,
I can't, I can't,
so, I run.

You find me in the study where we always went to pray.
It is dark now.
The window is a mirror of my face and passing traffic glare.
The world magnified by shame.

I can't turn around, and so,
you come to me–
cup my chin.

It is only your eyes,

You see who I am now, then.

A good mother,
Teacher of troubled youth,
The poet, writing these words for you.

I went home and later
to a different meeting than you.
My pride, when you broke our pact,
you were dating someone new.

Fifteen years after your death
I received a call.
She said it was always us, but
I always knew...that

If I could only go back,
I would meet you on the stairs
of our Philadelphia,

And, I would,
not let go.

Yo.

Eight Ball Corner Pocket

I wasn't looking for the me
from way back when, but
you were there,

Wearing that grin
in a back alley
bar in Charleston.

There, to the left of the entrance
in a dim lit corner,
the little Lefty.

One look, and I knew
you still had it.

Here's to Lisa
with a pool cue
no one could run
a game on you.

At first, it felt sinful
recalling those days long passed,
how you rolled a joint with ease
sitting on the stairs

At St. Boniface,
the sun parting the clouds
basking your youthful
light.

Like Christ, you would
die for a friend,
go that mile,
share your last cigarette.

With liquor in your satchel,
your long hair shimmering with snow
you would hit that party row

trudging and escaping
the bad breaks of life's throw.

In the shapes of those teen years,
Dad working back to prison, and
mom lost to bipolar on the streets,

The earth was spinning
off its axis, and still
you would not
scratch.

In time, I knew
to have a shot
I had to let you go,
or so I thought.

But, tonight I see you
in every gray felt
turned green.

It was you
hitting the pavement,
knocking on doors until
every sibling knew home.

You working two jobs,
going to college, helping me
raise two daughters alone.

And, you see the soul
of every troubled student
at this teacher's door.

I should have known.

Now, I want you to trust me
I know that's hard for you.
Take my hand,
I will pull you through.

We have so many
more years to do.

Let's rack 'em
We will rack 'em.

Texas Hold Me

It's been awhile since I played a good game of Texas Hold 'Em, and even longer since I have dated a man.
I profess to be skilled at the first, and out of practice in the latter.

The Basics:

Any player knows the face value of the cards.
If I could choose a card to represent me—it would never be the Queen.
I detest power plays over people. Games are another matter.
I am most like the Jack of Hearts.
There are 16 definitions for the word jack and defining me—
is a feat I am still mastering.
I chose the heart because it is my best feature.

Before entering the game, I size up my opponents.
I never sit to the right of the big better out of the gate.
In dating, I have spent years in self-reflection to craft and refine the better woman.

Starting Line:

In Texas Hold 'Em, the first two cards are considered the preflop and are in the hole.
That none of the other players know what you have—
well that's your biggest strong suit—
regardless of their face value.

This is also true in sizing up a good match:
A man can appear to have great traits, but an Ace is actually the low card in some instances.
There are non-tolerables which can range from –
having a low regard for those less fortunate, dismay at an old person taking time to cross the street, or a dislike of dogs.

Midpoint:

The second betting round is known as the flop and
three cards are turned up. These cards are significant.

If I don't have much to go on for a poker hand,
I may resort to bluffing.

I always bluff if the 9 and 3 show up on the flop.
It is a tactic that has no sound strategy, but I have walked away the
big winner when using it at least 70% of the time.

I am a horrible bluffer when it comes to dating.
I am the opposite of a game player.
I might look away intentionally, so my eyes don't give me up.
I am a woman of truth to my own detriment.
For the right person, this will make me more interesting.

Pre-Final:

At the turn, also known as 4th street, the stakes are
starting to escalate at the game table.
Many players have invested a lot and, then, ultimately folded.
By now, you know if your hand has winning potential–
unless you are a risk taker and waiting on that final river card.
It could be sink or swim

At this point, a man might know:

I like playing songs on old bridges,
I sometimes run late,
hug slim chances,
and believe in prayer and fate.
I spell love in foggy windows, and
I like a walk to my car to remind me that chivalry is not dead.

The Final Round:

The Jack of Hearts could be the River card if you take
your chances, showing up before all bets are off
and the chips are down.

In the game, that could complete a Flush, Full House,
or a Royal Straight, and I would be sitting pretty.

In dating, I've watched and waited on the sidelines
because I just couldn't sacrifice the dream.
It's always been nothing or everything.

So, if I go all in, and show my hand
someone will walk away...a Lucky man.

Love in a Rearview Mirror

My car knows the way
to the beach,
I am just a passenger

Thinking of a man I kissed
last winter,
how everything stopped.

How I could travel
his body
like a trip around the world

On leather seats,
parked at dusk,
in the backways
of a Carolina marsh.

It could have been so beautiful,
We would have been so beautiful.

Alone, I am so beautiful,
passing cars
I turn the music up.

Dwelling

I went to the house
of memory
I folded it
thirty-four times

One fold
for each move
of my childhood

Like paper
I was flattened
by the weight of it

When my Mother died
I returned
to open it

The folds were gone
I ate it
to sustain me

For Steve Cabrera

S.O.S.

When I see you now, I see you with a pole extended over the
                                                    water
                                                    waiting
                        for a   fish

 you can brag about.

I made it to the ocean and am learning how to listen to a soul's
                        navigation
                            N
                W   E
                            S

                Under this sky full of stars
                I hardly recognize
                the woman of
                so long
                ago

I was flailing as a single mother emptying.

                            .

            .
                buckets…from life's deck…learning to

                S
                I
                N
                K…or…swim.

When you became my friend,---the one man
who stayed to be our —S.O.S.

to help me move in multiples to a bigger boat, a better spot,
closer to land, and you took
the empty place__and filled the <u>lives</u> of my daughters as a Godfather—
                    holding little hands by the pond, baiting hooks
                    for first time fishing,
                    strong arms to carry them
                    while they were sleeping,
                    father/daughter dancing, steering
                    them in a better direction
                    as you taught driving, college visiting,
                    and waving … goodbye.
Then, they sent out flares of their own—for an oil change,
                              could you check that tire,
                              it's a beautiful day for a walk
                              down the aisle.

You were even there for the "welcome to the world"
of my first grandchild.

Now, my boat is docked, and from the shore
I gaze out to the vast tides of time .

In the moonlit darkness, I look at stars shaped
like a fishing hook and know that God casted you in my direction.

                                        *
                                        *
                                        *
                                        *

                                              *

When You Become Facebook Friends With Your Former Writing Professor

You know that twenty years
passed is
closer than you thought

and you are far removed
from a girl waving
words from a window sill
afraid to be seen and

in the space of that ellipsis…

a woman emerged
who doesn't edit herself and

words are fully present tense
like birdsong
when I hug the sky.

For Denise Cabrera

Keepers of the List

They say every mother should have a list.
A way to stay on top of it all.
The list is a lie.

We waded: in laundry
                             late night feedings
                             ear infections, and
                             what's for dinner.

We divided: Cheerios
                             toys
                             turns for T.V. and
                             the front seat.

(mostly, we divided
ourselves into seven)   for work, and
                             home, and
                             school, and
                             projects, and
                             a last kiss, and
                             who didn't get cake.

We celebrated: every birthday
                             holiday
                             baptism
                             award at school
                             games won, and
                             he took a step, and
                             she lost a tooth
                             first dance, and
                             graduation.

We were healers: of skinned knees
of hurt feelings from a teacher, friend, or foe
let me take your temp
make some soup
did that dream scare you
is that a rasp

We waited: for first words
steps
report cards
until someone found a shoe
footsteps on the stairs
a car door on the drive.

We were listeners: about a day at school
of the voices from cartoon characters
for falls
ambulances
a ringing phone
silences, and
tears, and
for the words, "I love you."

How much we love them, I still don't know the answer.

'To infinity and beyond' and more than that.

I just know we did it and 'you have a friend in me.'

Now what's up ahead is finding the girls from
before they were born, and the women
after they've grown.

Meet me at my house,

                Let's try them on.

Tendril

Once there was a land,
the softest of clearing,
and there was a tendril

there, waiting
to burst at the seams,

there, waving
to the sky

under a canopy
of stars.

this one day flower,
in the safety of her
one day field,

she went to sleep.

glass fell through the sky
of an open window,

a giant blade chopped her down.

thinking she was dirt,
not mirth,

she hid underground.

haunted by the cries
of other tendrils,

she rose
to face the blade
stalking around.

"This is my earth."

"I am Mirth."

"I am Mirth."

then,
the one day flower
on the day of her field,

opened
towards the yielding light
of the stars.

A Walk With Grandma

I wish I might gather all the birds
for you and sit among the flowers.
We would laugh the day away, and
there we'd talk for hours.

I would tell you all the stories
of your grandmas from before,
you wouldn't care I said it twice,
you'd say, "Just tell us more."

We'd sing a song to Jesus,
maybe to a ladybug,
and look for rainbows in the sky
a promise from above.

Someday, you will remember
all the walks you had with me,
where we stopped to smell the flowers,
look at birds soar past the trees.

You will know how very special,
and each day I prayed for you,
and there among our flowers
all the birds will sing with you.

For my daughters

The First and the Last

Memories can merge when you have two
daughters

I should have written it all down.

Who wore what costume on that
halloween
What was the color: blue or green of her dress that
prom
Where has all the time
gone

How does a mother forget such
things

Someday you'll say sorting souvenir teeth from random
boxes

Flattened flowers falling from random pages of all those
books

Apart you can list all my failings, yet
turn

To each other
therein my heart
therein my hands
hold.

Together, you are my greatest love.

Girl in Bloom

When I ask for a walk to my car
it is to honor her.
She is me.

Under the light of the moon
you hold me now,
this girl in bloom.

Your eyes how they turn
when I walk in a room,
as if the day had just begun.

Under that gaze, I open a
blissful blush and innocence
petals, bouquet, and song.

Such fullness in existing.

Reminiscent of my heart aglow
that summer
over 10,000 days ago,

When I was sixteen,
When girl meets boy
under the light of the moon.

At the county fair,
we pledged a long distance devotion.
My friends were dating, yet

I had his letters.
Running to the box
a laughing flower.

In the throes of my affection,
I swiped twelve bucks and
jumped on a Greyhound bus.

Everything was a touch of hand,
a longing glance, and
one kiss from his rooftop before
my father picked me up.

This was a life before that night,
before glass fell through the first sky
and severed a chasm
to a great divide.

Her cassette had stopped
the songs long done,
asleep with her dreams
and first times to come,

She is me.

The terror pounced on her there,
a vice like grip
around her neck,

Echoes in this canyon
"I will surely die."

She woke in blood,
a hostage for three hours,
unspeakable syllables.

No exit.

She army crawls for miles
to a back porch next door,
the devil would bow to this grief.

She is a specimen, photos
and interviews, and all the vessels
broke in her face.

She is me.

Can we pause,
I want to stop.
I am the girl

Who writes her name in the sand,
plays among the birds,
and prays at church.

I am a poet
sorting through the moons
to tell this story.

Falling off the edge of fear
was a nightly ritual for years.
In darkness,
she could hear the grass grow.

Run, run, run,
safer out than in,
she slept in the car
keys in her hand.

There were not enough drugs,
she tried a one night stand.
A body held by a Vietnam vet

Detour from the land mines,
the crawl,
the search for light,
so much in common.

Stop, I am this girl
keeping step beside you.

I play in the rain,

skip long farewells, and
open my arms to the sky.

It took twelve years
to get the call,
he had been locked up
for a decade.

She was never informed.
Never knew that answer.

Finally, there was a trial.

The police lost the evidence,
lost body under the bright lights,
lost envelope
lost girl, woman, and child.

They only have her photo
The eyes, her eyes, my eyes
broken silhouette of summer.

I climbed into them.
I went to the press.
I carried her with me.

We won,
we won,
we won.

April Fool's day–1993:
"We regret to inform you…
the state supreme court
overthrew the conviction."

Muted life
Where can I find you?

Then, the final call.

There were others, other girls, now women.
They are across the U.S.
on my side of the divide.

I am touching Braille in the dark,
someone knows my language.

We go together
One more trial,
Guilty, guilty, guilty

One hundred years.

We save someone, somewhere.
Somewhere a life is waiting,
somewhere it is summer.

Now, here I am.
Beside you
Here, now
under the light of the moon.

Jesus said..." the Lily in the field toileth not."
I reach for you
without pretense or thought,

I hold your face
in these two hands,
we kiss tenderly.

I feel so lucky, and
all of the good things
have finally caught up to me.

Out on a Limb

Once a terror broke in
this house collapsed inside
myself, and I had to
rebuild a universe.

In the void of that dark
God showed me the Orion
and a thousand stars
like candles by my window.

The sun rose again
and flowers unfurled
in the faces
of my children.

I journeyed and
swam with orcas
by canoe, touched the
Spirit on the water, and

Held the hand
of Mother Mary
in a remote
Montana church.

I felt the awe of the Son
on painted walls, saw
a wooden cross
and a little papoose.

I fed deer
in winter, touched
twilight on the snow
and slept safely again
under the stars
dying embers.

Yes, I have known
such splendor in
my solitary rooms.

Yet, tonight I have scaled
how days turned into years
and climbed out on a limb
under the silver moon.

In the distance, I hear
the sound of music
and remember that
I am a woman.

I am morning birdsong
The mountain and a valley
A field of wildflowers, and
Wind through the pines.

I am the last soft snowfall, and
The long dusk of summer's evening,
A sandy shore and
Recurring tide.

I am the stone unturned
Fragrance of a life with rough edges
A cool night's breeze, and the
Current of an ever flowing river...

With a passion never kindled
to set it all on fire.

Is there a man brave enough
to see the universe?

Strong enough
to hold the universe?

I am climbing off this bough,
I think it's time.

Finding Time

Is it all rushing by so fast?
This life, how it somehow got away.
If I might ask,
Could you go to your mind's eye?

Look! There, on that hill far away
to the wondrous time of childhood.
Here, where the longest of days are etched like fossil
and that one lone feather.

There you are
blustery among the walls of lasting joy~
Where anything is possible.

Where a ship on the highest sea
set off from a sidewalk puddle, and
a paper roll-the telescope
to view that faraway star.

See the stage~
How you traveled to those big, bright moons.

Can you tell me when we put boundaries around the journey?
Is this how we lost track of time?

Somehow in the pretense of our maturity
we lost the immeasurable tangibility
of the ever present... now.

Stop. Turn around.
Pick up time from the rushing pile
among all things commonplace.

There is still the longest afternoon.
How it waits for you,
before the glow of a corner streetlamp calls.

Savor the taste of that round, ripe peach.
Find your friends, make a pact,
forge anew to an unknown path.
Roll down a hill and laugh,
just laugh.

You might hold again that long ago truth,
you are invincible.

I wish you might find me there
along your road
among the crowd of faces,

with a kind word, an unwavering glance,
recall the touch of hand,
leaving that lasting, indelible impression.

Here and now..you are
life's shining promise.

Look to the stars.
See your silhouette,
the stage...

the moon is waiting.

Making My Entrance

There is a path behind me
it once called me by an alias.
I was on the run there
huddled like stone.

There among the ruins
I would rise up
for the truth
not black or white,

It is a narrow road
to living color.

I am my Mother's daughter.

I open the gate
to a quiet beach, and
hold the sky like flowers.

I write my name in the sand.

Guardian

Whom amongst the angels
was my charge

while slaying dragons there
among the sparrows?

you must lay down thy sword~

the greatest of these

is love.

About the author

Lisa Spears is from Peoria, Illinois and spent most of her life in the midwest. She resides in Charleston, SC and currently teaches English at Daniel Jenkins Academy to high school students experiencing trauma. She received her Master's of English degree at Western Illinois University in 2007 and her Master's of Fine Arts degree at Eastern Washington University in 2017. She is a single mother of two daughters and has three granddaughters. She moved to Charleston to pursue her writing career and live by the ocean. You can reach her by email at Follypoet63@gmail.com

Photo by Jason Layne